Faith in the Midst

A JESUS THRU THE LENS SERIES

Tanya Y. Hines

Copyright @ 2024 Tanya Y. Hines

First Edition

ISBN: 978-0-578-84326-1

All Rights Reserved.

Cover Photo Artwork: Rodney A. Ward

The contents of this book may not be reproduced, duplicated, or transmitted in any form, or by any means, electronic, photocopying, mechanical, recording, or otherwise, without direct, prior written permission of the author.

Disclaimer: All attempts have been made by the author to provide factual and accurate content. Information and advice in this book are to be followed at the discretion of the reader.

Dedication

This book is dedicated to the memory of my beloved mother, Margaret Ward, whom I miss each day and will always love.

Thank you, Mom, for teaching me how to have faith in the Lord and how to trust and keep moving despite the circumstances.

Thank you for teaching me how to love, be brave, and compassionate. Most importantly, thank you for teaching me how to encourage others; that developed my spiritual gift.

You are forever etched in my heart and soul.

Photo Credit: Tanya Y. Hines

A Special Message for You

As an author, I hope and pray with each book the Lord allows me to write, you always receive a message of the hope, grace, and love that our heavenly Father has for each of us. "Faith in the Midst" is designed to encourage you to keep moving, praising, and trusting as you navigate through the various seasons of your life. It's also to remind you that you are not alone, that life happens to each of us, but our God is so much greater than our life circumstances, and with him we will always be victorious!

My earthly walk has been a walk of faith, and without it I do not think I would be who I am today, nor would I have survived the turbulent seasons of life. The "Faith in the Midst" chapters are personal, and I hope they will inspire you to keep believing and trusting in the Lord through your own stories. Faith allows you to grow, have joy and even peace during the trials. It allows you to keep fighting and believing in the One who is greater.

The images in this book depict many variations of butterflies. Butterflies have been known to symbolize transformation, resurrection, life, hope, beauty, and peace. It is my prayer that you will connect with the attributes of the butterfly as you view the pictures and take in the mini faith chapters. May they both minister to your spirit.

Keep the faith!

Contents

1	You are Beautiful	1
2	A Godly Relationship	5
3	Infertility	10
4	Mother, Gone Too Soon	14
5	The "C" Word	19
6	Obedience	27
7	Faith	32
8	Shelter in Place	37
9	Hello Sunshine	42
10	Chosen by God	46

Photo Credit: Tanya Y. Hines

"Charm is deceptive, and beauty is fleeting; but a woman who fears the Lord is to be praised."

—PROVERBS 31:30 (NIV)

YOU ARE BEAUTIFUL

You are indeed beautiful. God created you to be you, special and loved. I can remember not believing, as a young girl, that I was beautiful. I was that tall, dark, skinny girl in the class, taller than most of the girls and even some of the boys. Always wanting and wishing I was shorter, lighter, and prettier. I was a young girl walking around with her head down and shoulders slumped because I couldn't see what others saw in me. Added to the lack of self-confidence were also traits of shyness.

We live in a world where society teaches us at a young age that we should not be happy with how God created us but should strive instead to look like the images that bombard our eyes and mind on television and social media. The constant messages that tell us that our hair should be a certain way, our weight should be lower, our shape should be smaller, teeth whiter, lips thinner or thicker, lashes longer, nose smaller, breasts bigger—the list is never-ending. So we, in many instances, keep striving to reach and obtain the world's image of beauty. That worldly focus becomes draining and depressing because the reach is too far to obtain.

I am thankful that God blessed me with a mother who saw the onset of low self-esteem driving the perception of who I thought I was.

We all need to have a Margaret Ward in our lives to motivate, love, and instill confidence. She taught me that God made me beautiful and in his image: "So God created mankind in his own image, in the image of God he created them, male and female, he created them" (Genesis 1:27 NIV). When we walk around with shoulders slumped, not walking proud and not loving ourselves, we are not honoring God. The Lord did not make a mistake when he created you: "Before I formed you in the womb, I knew you, before you were born, I set you apart" (Jeremiah 1:5 NIV). Imagine that: God thought of you before you were conceived and knew before you were born, who you would one day become. With love and tender care, he made an original design called You. I was always told that "God doesn't make junk," and I believe that's true. So how do we grab hold of the idea that I am beautiful and I am enough and stop allowing the world to make us feel inadequate? How do we stop striving to be something that we are not? Well, I would like to offer this suggestion to you: we conquer the doubts and inadequacies by taking our eyes off the worldly things and fixing them on the beauty and love that God has for us. When we begin to see ourselves through the "God lenses," we begin to recognize just how special we are and how much we are loved. A true awakening to God makes you realize that you were created in love by him and in his image. This reality in God dissolves feelings of not being good enough. When you understand that God loves you just as you are, you stop striving to answer the world's call, and you look to the one who created you with everlasting love and care. Beauty can be defined in so many ways, but true beauty comes from within and spreads outward. If your heart, mind, soul, and spirit are in alignment with the Lord, you cannot help but radiate beauty, joy, and peace. You are beautiful because you are a child of the King, and that's something to be proud of. So, beautiful you, let the world see you shine!

YOU ARE BEAUTIFUL
Thoughts & Reflections

Photo Credit: Tanya Y. Hines

> "But as for me, I watch in hope for the Lord, I wait for God my Savior; my God will hear me.
>
> —MICAH 7:7 (NIV)

A GODLY RELATIONSHIP

A godly relationship is something special and desired by God. We all desire to love and to be loved but at what cost? The Word tells us in (Song of Songs 8:4 NIV), "Daughters of Jerusalem, I charge you: Do not arouse or awaken love until it so desires." There is a spiritual reason for the Word reminding us not to awaken love before it's time: in our rush to love and be loved, we leave God out and cancel God's plans for us.

Love should not have to be coerced or forced; it should come easily. In order to attract the right kind of love, you must first have a high regard for yourself. This will keep you from settling and choosing someone who will be good to you. It takes time to first learn to love ourselves before others can begin to love us correctly.

There was a time in my life when, in retrospect, I know I lacked self-love. At that time, I attracted the wrong boys and men. Teenage boys did not give me the respect that I deserved but rather cheated, lied, and disrespected me. Did I know deep down in my spirit that it wasn't right? Yes, but I hadn't built enough self-love to stand my ground and say, "This is not right! I deserve better and if you cannot do better, I will not be part of this relationship." Waking love before it's time was the result of my poor choices as a young teenage girl. I truly believe that high schoolers should not attach titles like "boyfriend" and "girlfriend" to their friendships and should just be friends. Titles bring confusion and usually disappointment at that tender age because you are trying to awaken love when you are still in the process of grappling with growing and trying to understand who you are. The dynamics of relationships at an early age can sometimes filter into our future relationships as we matriculate from teenage years to adult. I can recall times in my early adult years of still not loving myself the way God loves and sees me, and that caused me to continue in a cycle of wrong choosing. I guess some would label me as that "good girl" who picked the "bad boys." In that wrong choosing, you risk inviting emotional and physical abuse and not being treated like the daughter of the King that you are. It came to a point where I clearly heard the Lord tell me to take a step back and not date anyone so that I could analyze the choices that I was making. During that hiatus period I realized I was not loving myself in a manner that would be pleasing to God. The Lord began to convict my spirit on the things I was doing and allowing to be done to me. In that revelation of understanding and declaring that I deserved better, I attracted better and met a guy who would soon become my husband of now, 30 years. I remember talking to God and saying, "I'm not doing a good job at this dating thing, so I am going to not date and allow you to choose for me." That was the best decision I could have ever made! (Proverbs 18:22 NIV) says that "He who finds a wife finds what is good and receives favor from the Lord." If I could add to that, I would say that she who waits on the Lord to allow him to bring the one he has ordained for her finds favor, happiness, peace and, yes, joy from the Lord in her union.

    A godly relationship is not devoid of problems because there are two humans who make up that relationship, and we are imperfect. However, with God in the midst of that union, there will certainly be more good than bad. A godly relationship, I believe, can be defined as one where God has caused two paths to cross at an ordained time and place and will allow that meeting to develop into what he has planned.

Waiting on a godly relationship takes faith and patience. However, if you love yourself the way God loves you, you will not be tempted to settle for anything less than what God has decreed for you. A true godly relationship is well worth the delay, and in your wait, remember (Hebrews 6:15 NIV): "And so after waiting patiently, Abraham received what was promised." You too will receive your promise if you trust and depend on the Lord and do not awaken love before it's the right time.

A GODLY RELATIONSHIP
Thoughts & Reflections

Photo Credit: Tanya Y. Hines

"I will trust in the Lord with all my heart and lean not on my own understanding."

—PROVERBS 3:5 (NIV)

3

INFERTILITY

Many people view the subject of infertility as something that should not be discussed or shared, especially with strangers. It's a topic that carries pain, embarrassment, jealousy, a loss of hope or faith, and in many instances a distancing from God. Infertility is something that I've experienced firsthand. My wonderful and blessed husband and I had to face one of our first tough battles about five years into our marriage: the struggle and desire to become parents.

It's in times like these that having a godly marriage becomes a true benefit. Infertility issues can quickly destroy a marriage if it's not rooted and grounded in the Lord. My husband and I were not in a rush to have children, but when we made the decision that we were ready, it did not happen the way we expected. It would be a journey of five years and many infertility doctors' visits before we would conceive. During that five-year period, I had many high and low moments.

The journey began with a lot of hope, yet it transitioned into anger and jealousy, and then faith and hope would kick back in and win the battle. I am thankful to God that my trust in him was strong enough to sustain me. With much prayer and faith, I began to trust the Lord for what I was asking. Scripture tells us in (Romans 4:17 NIV) that God "gives life to the dead and calls into being things that are not." I had to learn to trust God and believe God against all doctors' reports. I had to believe that the desire of my/our hearts would be fulfilled by our heavenly Father.

Faith had to kick into overdrive for me to walk through this, but once it did nothing could shake it, and that would be a good thing. Once I'd conceived, I started out with twins, but only one would make it through the pregnancy and birth. One embryo spontaneously aborted, but my son was able to fight through all the challenges during the pregnancy. Nine months of complete bed rest and back- to-back health challenges never caused my faith to wane. I believed God and defeated the enemy's attacks with the Word of God. There have been certain moments in my life that I have been a true faith giant, and this was one.

I was locked and loaded on the promises of God. The doctors couldn't scare me; my own body fighting against me wouldn't deter me, and being in my bed for nine months wouldn't break me. This season in my life was faith at its highest!

Often, we look at our challenges as breaking points, but I believe a lot of our challenges are permitted by God so that he can help us mature in our faith. If we were devoid of challenges, we would never know how strong our faith muscles are and can become. It is through the hardships, the unexpected happenstances, the health reports, etc. that we look more closely to God for answers.

Challenging circumstances in life remind us of the higher power that resides in us that will cause us to triumph if we glean from it. The "tap on the shoulder" from God points us back to him. Just like our earthly parents, our heavenly Father wants us to come to him for comfort, answers, and relief: "Come to me, all you who are weary and burdened, and I will give you rest" (Matthew 11:28 NIV). You too can experience God's peace in the midst of your storms. Just call on his name, saturate yourself in his Word, and know that the building of your faith will see you through.

INFERTILITY
Thoughts & Reflections

Photo Credit: Tanya Y. Hines

"You, Lord are my lamp; the Lord turns my darkness into light."

—2 SAMUEL 22:29 (NIV)

4

MOTHER, GONE TOO SOON

December 11, 2015, is a day that I shall never forget. It is the day my mother, Margaret Ward, went home to be with the Lord at the young age of 77. My mother was so full of life and youthfulness before dementia dimmed her world. She could walk into a room, and her beauty and grace would saturate the area, but the disease slowly stole that from her.

This disease is so dark because it can literally transform a person into an unrecognizable being. I often would look at her and in my mind quietly ponder: Whose mother is this? She certainly cannot be mine! Where is that woman who was always so well put together, so charming, energetic, meticulous, and full of praise? How could this dreadful disease rob her of everything that she once was?

Watching a loved one fight this disease can be very agonizing. It's frustrating and sad to see them slowly morph into a state of unknowing. *Are you my mother?* I thought. I would look deep into her eyes, and I could actually see the dimness expanding. The confusion, forgetfulness, frustration, and paranoia had now become her everyday reality.

Her desire to have her hair washed and combed, to be bathed, and her ability to impeccably dress all faded as the disease progressed.

Weakness, confusion, and a mean spirit would often be part of her new reality.

I would watch my mother fail to even recognize herself, often talking to the "woman in the mirror." Most people would say she was just babbling, but the times that I was able to witness this strange behavior, I quickly realized not all words were babble. I could tell her mind would drift back to her youth and times of previous fears or even demons that she had dealt with. She would warn the "woman in the mirror" and even me of things that her mind was focused on at that time. I discovered some things about my mother that she had not shared with me previously during these moments of so-called babble. My heart would ache for her because there wasn't anything I could really do to help her, other than try to be with her in that unknown space. Oh, how I prayed for her deliverance from this dreadful disease. I wanted God to restore her mind and body to what it once had been. My faith told me that although the doctor's report said that she would continue to decline, nothing was too hard for the God I serve.

I saw my mother beat many other attacks on her body and health over the years that ranged from a near-death car accident to bladder cancer, and I was expecting to witness another healing miracle in her life in this trial. (Psalm 103:2-3 NIV) tells us to "Praise the Lord, my soul, and forget not all his benefits who forgives all your sins and heals all your diseases." I stood and focused on the *all* your diseases' in this verse. We know that God's word does not return to us void and that His promises are the promises of yesterday, today, and tomorrow, so in faith I believe that healing always does occur, but it doesn't always materialize in the manner we hope and desire.

When the Lord called my beloved mother home, at that moment, her healing occurred. She was relieved from the anguish and suffering of her illness. My hope was that the healing would occur on this side of heaven so that I could physically have her with me still, watch her shout, praise, and testify how God had delivered her yet again, but that did not happen. Her healing came on the other side of heaven when her heavenly Father called her to now be with him: "To be absent from the body, is to be present with the Lord" (2 Corinthians 5:8 NIV). I try to trust God in all things with the understanding that our earthly diseases and sicknesses may be overwhelming to us, but they aren't to God. There is not one disease that can baffle God. He can heal every one of them if he so chooses.

My sisters and brothers, healing does happen; we just are not always able to witness it work out in the life of our loved ones. I encourage you to keep trusting, believing, and praying. God hears your heart's desire. "This is the desire we have in approaching God, if we ask anything according to his will, he hears us" (1 John 5:14 NIV), "At sunset, the people brought to Jesus all who had various kinds of sickness, and laying hands on each one, he healed them." (Luke 4:40 NIV)

MOTHER, GONE TOO SOON
Thoughts & Reflections

Photo Credit: Tanya Y. Hines

"So do not fear, for I am with you; do not be dismayed, for I am your God. I will strengthen you and help you; I will uphold you with my righteous right hand."

—ISAIAH 41:10 (NIV)

5

THE "C" WORD

The "C" word... CANCER! People dread hearing a diagnosis for themselves or their loved ones that involves cancer. It often invokes fear, depression, and/or anger. In others, it stirs up faith, fight, and hope to conquer the enemy that has invaded the body. My first encounter with cancer was in my early twenties, when I was informed that I had first-stage cervical cancer. Fear, of course, swept over me at the mention of this. I wondered, *How? Why? Would I live?* I looked to my doctor to answer all these questions for me. At this time in my life, I knew the Lord, but I was not walking closely with him, and that really makes a difference in how you process things. I remember being sad and afraid, but my doctor reassured me that a simple procedure would most likely solve the issue. One of the blessings in this was that it was in its early stage and didn't require me to have to go through any treatments other than an in-office surgical procedure. My faith back then was not the faith that I currently have, but after the procedure was done and a few years had passed, I didn't fear cervical cancer any longer. I followed the doctor's advice and did my exams every six months and then eventually went back to the annual exam.

As time passed and I reflect, I did operate in faith because I never thought or felt like I would get that diagnosis again. I didn't have a fear of going to the doctor, but I was diligent and still am about making sure I get checked every year. The Lord was with me, and I am grateful for that. I never thought about the cancer; it was as if I almost forgot about it until I needed to fill out medical forms that asked me about my health history.

Fast forward to 2017, and once again, cancer decided to rear its ugliness in my body. This time it was first-stage breast cancer, but the difference is that, by now, I was very strong in my faith. It also came at a time where there had been significant back-to-back challenges in my life. The death of my mother, my son's major sports injury and surgery, the death of my mother-in-love, major business losses, and other health challenges tried to attack me physically and mentally. In May of 2017, I had to deal with having breast cancer surgery.

Battling life can sometimes make us weary, especially if we allow it to do so, but we've got to keep fighting. I am always that optimistic patient who boldly confesses to my doctor that I am not worried about the things they tell me; I trust God for my reports to come back in my favor. Unfortunately, this time it did not. Instead, the report came back as cancer. As I sat on my doctor's table, tears of disbelief slipped from my eyes. "No," I said. "I have been declaring to my prayer group that I know I am healed," so this could not be, but it was!

My faith muscles were already pumped from all the other challenges mentioned previously, but I did not think I would ever have to deal with this particular fight *again*. I left my doctor's office and sat in my car to process the news, and I remember speaking out loud to the Lord asking, "So now what do you want me to say about this report?" I clearly heard him say, *Keep saying and believing what you've already been declaring.* I did just that as I dialed my husband's number to tell him the news. I am so thankful to the Lord for giving me a measure of faith that stays in the forefront even in a trial. I remember telling the Lord, okay, that's what I am going to do, so I will walk through this in a manner that no one will know, not even my own son. I remember laying out to the Lord what I was believing in faith this journey would look like. I said, "So Lord, I am believing you for the victory, and I will not lose my hair. I will not be sick or look sick from treatments. I will look my very best, keep my joy, peace, and praise you. I will trust you and keep my hope, and more than that, I will be an angel to someone going through this who doesn't have the hope and faith that I have." The scripture that inspired me during this time was (Ephesians 3:20 NIV): "Now to him who is able to do immeasurably more than all we ask or imagine, according to his power that is at work within us."

Yes, I was asking God for some big stuff and then trusting him for immeasurably more, and yes, he delivered it all. I was blessed through six weeks of radiation treatments five days a week. No one knew what I was going through except a very small handful of people. I didn't want to burden my only child with the news of this because he was in his last two years of high school, and I wanted him to enjoy this time of his life and not be worried about his mother. It was my decision to protect him and others by not telling them about my ordeal.

During my treatments, I met someone who was battling stage 4 cancer, and I was able to be a disciple and bring him to the Lord. It's amazing how the Lord works. I went in looking for someone who looked more like me, a female, to help and bring hope. However, God said no, it will be a Caucasian male who has been out of church for over sixty years. The friendship and support that he and I developed will last a lifetime. During one of our many times of fellowship, he told me that I was an angel to him. Those were the exact words that I asked the Lord to bless me with when I asked him to show me someone who needed to see Christ in the midst of this medical storm. He honored my prayer and desire, and I was able to bless a very special person.

During this season of my life, I also felt the presence of God, and that allowed me to have a glow, high spirits and to just look my best even though I was going through this ordeal. God delivered every one of my requests and more. Faith goes a long way to get you to victory! Being wiser in my faith, I knew not only to declare my victory over this prognosis but also to declare and decree that it would never come back in my life in any form in Jesus's name! I am trusting God to keep me cancer-free for the rest of my days! My trust in the Lord is according to (Jeremiah 17:7 NIV) "But blessed is the one who trusts in the Lord, whose confidence is in him" and (Hebrews 11:1 NIV) "Now faith is confidence in what we hope for and assurance about what we do not see." The enemy is cunning! Cancer round three: I truly believed cancer would not touch me again, so instead of attacking me, the enemy attacked my husband in December of 2018 with cancer. Back-to-back attacks on me and my family. I had been battling the enemy over so many things, and now a new battle was dawning.

In all honesty, this news rocked my world for a moment. I could not believe my ears when my husband had to share his report with me. It had been only a year earlier that my husband was supporting me on my journey, and now the script had flipped. I remember looking at my husband, who had a more aggressive form than I did, and saying that my son and I needed him, and he had to beat this. My rock was being rocked. I also remember confessing to the Lord, *I am tired, Lord, tired of fighting and battling issues.* It has been five years of sequential major problems. Once again, I heard the Lord say, well, if you are tired of fighting, daughter, then the enemy wins... Checkmate!

I thought, *no this cannot happen! Let me snap out of this real quick and put my battle clothes back on! Faith muscles let's get ready for a new workout!* And so, the battle continued, and I leaned on (Jeremiah 31:25 NIV) "I will refresh the weary and satisfy the faint" and (Galatians 6:9 NIV) "Let us not become weary in doing good, for at the proper time we will reap a harvest if we do not give up." My husband and I, in faith, trusted God to bring him through like he had done for me. He has walked this journey in a very blessed manner.

I was honored to be by his side through his treatments just as he was with me. Then, suddenly, I wasn't allowed to attend the treatments any longer because of the Covid-19 pandemic. No longer was I by his side, but God most certainly was, keeping him safe and protecting him from being infected while at the hospital twice a month in the middle of the pandemic. We again chose to keep the experience quiet because it's important that people view you as you see yourself. If you tell people you have cancer, many times they automatically think the worst because cancer can be bigger than their faith. We also chose not to burden our son with his father's diagnosis for the same reason as before. Now that he was a freshman in college, we wanted his time there to be all about him and not us. If I say I am well and I act well, others will view me as well. If I say I am sick and act sick, others will view me as sick. We wanted people to see us as we saw ourselves—, completely healed!

We are both more mature in faith, and we continue to believe and trust God for deliverance. We now proclaim cancer shall not come near us again or anyone in our household and stand on (Psalm 91:1-2 NIV) "He who dwells in the shelter of the Most High will rest in the shadow of the Almighty. I will say to the Lord, "He is my refuge and my fortress, my God, in whom I trust." (Jeremiah 32:27 NIV) "I am the Lord, the God of all mankind. Is anything too hard for me?"

I also realize that if we are here on earth, we will have to continue to fight the good fight of faith because the enemy will always want to trip us up and cause us to doubt what the Lord has for each of us. The key is that even in the midst of any storm, we keep the faith. We are God's battling warriors, and he has given us an advantage of fighting *from* victory because of the cross and not *to* victory. The fight is already won. We must simply believe and act by faith. So, whatever you are faced with, my journey was cancer but yours may be something else--you have the victory! Keep the faith and keep believing in the Word of the Lord and remember (Romans 4:17 NIV) reminds us that it is God who gives life to the dead and calls into being things that were not and (1 Corinthians 15:57 NIV) states "But thanks to God! He gives us the victory through our Lord Jesus Christ."

THE "C" WORD
Thoughts & Reflections

Photo Credit: Tanya Y. Hines

"If you obey my commands, you will remain in my love, just as I have obeyed my Father's commands and remain in His love."

—JOHN 15:10 (NIV)

6

OBEDIENCE

1 Samuel 15:22 (NIV) tells us, "Does the Lord delight in burnt offerings and sacrifices as much as in obeying the Lord? To obey is better than sacrifice, and to heed is better than the fat of rams." Many times, the Lord gives us a vision or a task to do, and we sit on it instead of moving towards it. I like to call it those "God assignments and projects" that I too am very guilty of being stagnant. There have been times in my life when I have clearly and without a doubt heard the Lord tell me to do something, yet I didn't do it. Was it out of disobedience, fear, or self-doubt that I did not move toward the goal and assignment given?

I would probably say *yes* to all the above. Disobedience in a lot of instances is not out of a sheer desire not to obey the Lord; instead, it is from the enemy who has convinced us we are not worthy or equipped for the call. My "God assignment" was the first book that I published, *Jesus Thru the Lens*, which was given to me well over three decades ago, but it was born only two years ago. I have always enjoyed taking photos, and the Lord told me to take those photos and make them speak about how God loves and wants to inspire us in our everyday surroundings.

Without a shadow of a doubt, I knew this was my assignment, yet I sat on it for almost 30 years. Oh, the things we tell ourselves to keep us in that familiar, safe, and comfortable place. My voices were, *your pictures are not good enough, who would want to hear your words of encouragement, you don't know anything about writing a book*, and so on. I thought about it, spoke about it, prayed about it, yet did nothing. I often would even tell the Lord, *I know I need to complete this, and I don't want you to call me home when I still have not done it and have you ask me why.* The thought of having to meet my Savior and stand before him knowing I was disobedient was something I continuously wrestled with.

I had no real peace in my stagnancy, so in 2019 I decided to trust God and just do it. That was one of the most fulfilling things I have ever done. The joy of being obedient to the vision was elating. To have the book out and published has been such a blessing and very humbling. The blessed feedback about *Jesus Thru the Lens* has served as confirmation that God's calling was not a mistake, and in hindsight I believe the delay in my writing the book also was preordained. He planted the seed; the seed was being watered over the years; it grew, and when it was ready, it bloomed. I honestly believe that it took time because over those many years, my relationship with the Lord grew. Also, my life experiences elevated my faith and my trust in him. (1 Timothy 1:1 NIV) states, "I thank Christ Jesus our Lord, who has given me strength, that he considered me trustworthy, appointing me to his service" and (Proverbs 3:5 NIV) "Trust in the Lord with all your heart and lean not on your own understanding" were scriptures that helped me move forward.

What has God spoken to you about? What is that assignment that the Lord has asked you to do in a way that no other person can implement? What is the enemy whispering in your other ear? Whose voice is louder? I urge you not to allow the voice of self-doubt or fear to hinder what the Lord has placed in you. If God spoke to you, then he's also going to give you everything needed to accomplish it.

(Exodus 9:16 NIV) says, "But I have raised you up for this very purpose, that I might show you my power and that my name might be proclaimed on earth." I am a true testimony to this. It's by the sheer grace of God that my first book is published. Now I am writing this one and it feels so good to know that I am walking in my purpose to encourage others through my words and photographs. When you wait, it doesn't mean that you cannot still fulfill the calling, but you may experience some regrets. Yes, it is true, as I've just stated, that while I was stuck, I underwent some spiritual growing lessons that were useful to my completing the assignment, but there were also some regrets. One of the major regrets that I personally have is the fact that my mother did not live to see me finally complete and publish my books. I would love to have seen her face as I presented them to her. That is a joy that I will never experience because she's no longer with me in the flesh. I do, however, believe that she is in heaven smiling down upon me and cheering me on as she's always done.

If you are obedient, you won't have regrets. For that reason, I want to encourage you to move forward. Don't worry about the naysayers or even the one inside you; you can accomplish all that God has placed in you. He didn't give you the vision for it not to be finished. I urge you not to wait any longer- Start Today! Piece by piece, moment by moment, and task by task is how you begin. Most importantly, just begin. Once you do, it will be one of the best moments you'll experience, to know you are doing what God has gifted you with and instructed you to do. God's word in (Romans 11:29 NIV) states "for God's gifts and His call are irrevocable" and in (Romans 12:6 NIV) "We have different gifts, according to the grace given to each of us." My beloved sisters and brothers, your "God adventure" awaits!

OBEDIENCE
Thoughts & Reflections

Photo Credit: Tanya Y. Hines

"If you have faith as small as a mustard seed, you can say to this mulberry tree, 'Be uprooted and planted in the sea, and l will obey you."

—LUKE 17:6 NIV

FAITH

We hear a lot about faith in the news, in church, and even on social media. Many of us recognize that it's a good attribute to have, but we often struggle when it's time to stand on it for ourselves. When the giants come knocking, can your faith withstand? I often testify that without faith and God in my life, I do not think I could have made it through the many trials and tests life has brought my way. Through the years my faith has gotten stronger, and I am sure it will continue to grow.

As you reflect on your life and see how the Lord has been there all the time, that will help your faith increase. It's also important to build your faith in the good times of your life, when things are going well and in the manner that you desire, because even then, faith in God is still very necessary. These are the times that we thank God for His divine order in our lives, and we should still spend time growing the Word in our hearts so that when the seasons shift, we have enough faith built to enter the battle season.

When the seasons reposition and we are faced with sicknesses, plagues like Covid-19, heartbreak, job loss, financial challenges and many other uncertainties, that's the time when the Lord watches to see how we maneuver in it. Will we, and can we, keep praising him and trusting him? Will we, and can we, pray without ceasing and trust that he hears and will answer? Will we, and can we, keep our peace and even find joy during the storm? Will we, and can we, even though we are hurting, help another? Challenging seasons will always show us our true selves. Sometimes, it's not who we think we see in the mirror. For some, we gain a godly strength that can only be deposited into us by God himself: "And he became more and more powerful, because the Lord God Almighty was with him" (2 Samuel 5:10 NIV); "I love you, Lord, my strength" (Psalms 18:1 NIV); "The Lord gives strength to his people; the Lord blesses his people with peace" (Psalms 29:11 NIV).

It's not easy when we are suffering, but God wants us to draw our strength and endurance from him. No, in and of ourselves we cannot fight the enormous battles of life, but God has told us that we are indeed more than conquerors: "No, in all of these things *stress, isolation, depression, anxiety, uncertainties, health, low self-esteem, plagues, and more we are more* than conquerors through him who loved us" (Romans 8:37 NIV).

God has given us everything we need to put the devil back into place, the pit of hell. It won't be an easy task, but the blood of Jesus Christ runs through our veins, and that blood never loses its power, which means we keep the power within us too. (Jeremiah 17:8 NIV) says, "They will be like a tree planted by the water that sends out its roots by the stream. It does not fear when heat comes; its leaves are always green. It has no worries in a year of drought and never fails to bear fruit." In today's lingo we say, "The struggle is real," and yes, that is true when we are engaged in spiritual warfare, but the victory belongs to Jesus, and it also belongs to you and me.

So, what happens when you're faced with a giant or giants and you look in the mirror and you don't see strength but weakness? Does this mean you lose the battle? Does this mean God has forgotten about you because you are in a fearful or unsteady state? Does it mean that he's mad because you are not strong? No! Not at all! God knows that we are human, and we do get weary at times. We have fought battle after battle, and when the fight is over, we have no more fight left within us. The tears are streaming down our faces, and our hearts are heavy. Joy and peace are distant memories. We believe we are at a point where there is nowhere to turn. Trust that God sees and knows exactly where you are spiritually and mentally, and the good news is that he has your back even in your moments of fragility and vulnerability. God himself said, "I will go before you and will be with you; I will never leave you nor forsake you. Do not be afraid; do not be discouraged" (Deuteronomy 31:8 NIV) (Isaiah 40:29 NIV) says, "He gives strength to the weary and increases the power of the weak." Finally, (2 Corinthians 12:9 NIV) says, "But he said to me, "My grace is sufficient for you, for my power is made perfect in weakness. Therefore, I will boast all the more gladly about my weaknesses, so that Christ's power may rest on me." I believe what the Lord wants his sons and daughters to do when we are in despair is to lean on him and trust that he'll pull us through. We serve a caring and loving God, a God who wants the best for us, who forgets and forgives all the mistakes and sins we have ever committed and will ever commit: "If we confess our sins, he is faithful and just and will forgive us our sins and purify us from all unrighteousness" (1 John 1:9 NIV).

So, as we navigate through those times of weakness, we are being renewed by God so that we will become strong again through his power and might. Our weaknesses diminish when we are looking up towards heaven and seeing God in all his splendor and glory, and there lies our strength to face another day, mountain, or obstacle. Be encouraged; faith in God and his abilities will spring you towards your victory and clothe you in your battle mentality and gear. The victory is yours!

FAITH
Thoughts & Reflections

Photo Credit: Tanya Y. Hines

"For in the day of trouble he will keep me safe in his dwelling; he will hide me in the shelter of his sacred tent and set me high upon a rock."

—PSALM 27:5 (NIV)

8

SHELTER IN PLACE

The year 2020 brought along with it a new phrase that many of us never had thought about before, and that phrase is "shelter in place." Shelter in place was a result of the 2020 international pandemic crisis of Covid-19. It was a time that placed most of us into isolation from the human touch and socialization. For many, this became a time of despair and hopelessness. To be sheltered in place not by choice but by government ordinance was difficult for many people. No one could have predicted in January that this would take place. To be cut off from family and friends and isolated was virtually unheard of, yet it became our new norm.

Unfortunately, many lives were lost—loved ones, friends, and friends of friends. Covid-19 challenged many people with their faith. Even those with the strongest faith had moments when faith felt like it was slipping. I count myself to be amongst those with strong faith, but Covid-19 made me fight to keep faith stronger than the pandemic. How does one maintain a strong faith as the entire world is experiencing a silent, invisible, and deadly predator that is taking people out every day, fight an invisible adversary, stand when the world around you seems to be crumbling bit by bit, and get away from this monster when everything is centered on it—the television, the radio, the news, and everyone's conversations?

The Bible even reminds us in (1 Peter 5:8 NIV) to "be alert and sober of mind. Your enemy the devil prowls around like a roaring lion looking for someone to devour."

Thank God the next verse (1 Peter 5:9 NIV), tells us to "Resist him, standing firm in the faith, because you know that the family of believers throughout the world is undergoing the same kind of sufferings." This was indeed a pandemic that touched believers and non-believers everywhere throughout the world. How does faith reign in days like this? Well, continuing with (1 Peter 5:10 NIV), we read, "And the God of all grace, who called you to his eternal glory in Christ, after you have suffered a little while, will himself restore you and make you strong, firm, and steadfast." That reminds us that Covid-19 and any other pestilence or infirmity is not going to last forever.

He will make sure that we are unmovable when we look to him for our restoration and strength. Faith that has been planted and watered will not falter when the heated challenges of life come our way. It may sway briefly, but it won't fail us. How do we keep the faith? We stay in faith by looking, listening, and seeking God to comfort, confirm, encourage, and remind us that he is bigger than that "thing" that plagues us: "You, Lord will keep the needy safe and will protect us forever from the wicked" (Psalm 12:7 NIV). Praise God, we are forever protected from the enemy. (Mark 11:22 NIV) Have faith in God, Jesus answered."

How does faith look on the other side of a pandemic? (Joshua 22:4 NIV), "Now that the Lord your God has given them rest as he promised, return to your homes in the land that Moses the servant gave you on the other side of Jordan." *I believe* that God would want us to come out better, stronger, and more faithful. Trials serve as opportunities to seek and grow in God. I don't believe God would want us to come out of the fire the same way we went into the fire. Our faith, most importantly, should be stronger because we've seen how God moved and protected us. We look more like God because we've hopefully seen the anointing he placed on us, and our faith muscles have increased because we've fought or "faithed" our way through.

Faith on the other side of the struggle places you in a stronger position to battle the next war and allows you to be more resilient. It is sweeter and more humbling because you've seen how the Lord has kept you and it also causes you to have more peace, praise, and shouts of joy. On the other side of the struggle, garners encouragement for others as they've watched your story unfold. Faith on the other side brings you closer to God and is victorious.

SHELTER IN PLACE
Thoughts & Reflections

Photo Credit: Tanya Y. Hines

"From the rising of the sun to the place where it sets, the name of the Lord is to be praised."

—PSALMS 113:3 NIV

9

HELLO SUNSHINE

I would like to imagine that each morning we wake, our heavenly Father is looking down upon us with that old familiar phrase "hello sunshine." But I would like to spell it as "Sonshine," for we are indeed his and made in his image. He awakens us with gifts, the gifts of life, new mercies, and provisions for the day. He's called us into another day of adventure to choose to walk with him every step of the way or go it alone and on our own. Every day that we are given is a true gift from God and we should handle it with care. Months and years are all filled with new days that we have only once, and then those days vanish into the past and are stored in our history. Today, at this moment, how are you handling your gift? Are you moving in anguish, impatience, fear, dread, doubt, and faithlessness? Or are you handling your gift with praise, joy, peace, faithfulness, trust, and confidence in the Gifter of the day? As God presents us with new days, he wants us to be excited, hopeful, and filled with anticipation. Like a child on Christmas morning who eagerly awaits dawn so they can run to the Christmas tree to see what good things are underneath, we, as God's sons and daughters, should have that same joy and anticipation with the dawning of the next day of life. Sometimes children express disappointment because they didn't get everything they had on the list or that one special gift that their parents couldn't afford, but that disappointment quickly fades in the wake of all the other good things they received. We too sometimes awaken sluggishly because we must face life that is sometimes hard and we are in the middle of another season of uncertainty, but if we can take on that childlike faith and see all the good things that God has in store for us and we can confront our day with the assurance that God is able and willing to see us through as stated in (Psalm 23:4 NIV), "Even though I walk through the darkest valley, I will fear no evil, for you are with me; your rod and your staff, they comfort me" and in (James 1:12 NIV), "Blessed is the one who perseveres under trial because, having stood the test, that person will receive the crown of life that the Lord has promised to those who love him."

God doesn't demand we appreciate life and choose to walk with him each day, nor that we serve him. He chose us first! (John 3:16 NIV) says, "For God so loved the world that he gave his one and only Son, that whoever believes in him shall not perish but have eternal life"; (1 Corinthians 2:12 NIV) says, "What we have received is not the spirit of the world, but the Spirit who is from God, so that we may understand what God has freely given us." The Gifter of the most precious gift you could ever receive, chooses to bless, love, care, and protect you. It is not mandatory for him to do so, but he does these things for us because he loves each one of us. We can take these precious gifts and remember to use them each day that we are blessed with. It is our choice; he will not ever force himself on us. So, choose today; your gifts are waiting...*Sunshine!*

HELLO SUNSHINE
Thoughts & Reflections

"And who knows but that you have come to your royal position for such a time as this."

—ESTHER 4:14

10

CHOSEN BY GOD

Chosen by God is a thought or statement that we often don't dwell on. It's in our natural human thought pattern to think God hasn't called me, hasn't chosen me. We assume that we are not chosen because we are unworthy, inadequate, not smart enough, not good enough, and not equipped. The truth of the matter is that if you are alive, have breath in your body, were born into this sinful world, then you were chosen by God. We all are chosen by God. Some of us have a purpose here on earth that is grand, and others have a smaller purpose, but one that is just as important and special to our heavenly Father. So, let's dive into this thought for a moment. To be chosen means that God thought about you, who you would become what you would endure, how you would impact the world, and even how long you would have on earth. He sees your life from beginning to end—from birth to death. Nothing can take him by surprise nothing is ever insurmountable for him. He knows the missteps and mistakes that we will make. He knows our hearts and our hearts' desires. He knows our fears, doubts, strengths, and our weaknesses. We cannot outwit him. He is all-knowing in every life that he has created. He decided when we would be born and even what we will live through in our lifetime. We have been chosen for such a time as this. Chosen to walk the earth now, the year of 2024. Chosen!

Since we are chosen, planned, and created by God, we also receive our strength and victory from God. It is all about God and not about us. It's a divine God plan!

I believe that if we could keep this thought in the forefront of our minds, we would have a different mindset and perspective of life in general. The good times will be even better if we remember that God has chosen us for this season. Many would say that living the desires of our hearts is the "good times." Having family and friends that love and care about us, having security, being in good health, being prosperous, and being in sound mind—with those, many would declare, "I'm living the good life." If we indeed are chosen by God, then the same would be so when times and seasons grow dim or dark. When our health declines, when our finances become challenging, and when life in general is turned upside down, we are still chosen by God. He's chosen us to walk through the darkness for this season. Why?

I believe that if the Lord allows things to enter our lives to disrupt them, he knows that we can handle them if we keep our attention focused on him and not the circumstances. He knows that he is more than enough to get us through. He knows that in him, we can endure. It's not too hard to persevere when we have our minds fixed on the Lord. By taking our concentration off the issue and placing God in the epicenter of our life, remembering we are chosen, we can walk in triumph.

Your mindset automatically shifts when you declare, "I am chosen by God." If he allowed this circumstance to enter our life, then he has planned how it will exit out our life as well. Chosen!

Chosen for such a time as this means I can and will handle it. The road may be long and tough, may dip, turn, twist, and be diverted, but if we are chosen, then we are girded for the challenges. To be chosen is to be selected or called. God selected us to grace the earth to be his light, provide encouragement, hope, and guide the lost and unsaved to him.

No situation we encounter in life is a surprise to God. Even in our free will, there are no surprises. Let this sink into your mind and spirit: whatever you may be facing today, God chose you, God is with you, God has equipped you, and God will never abandon you.

It took many years for me to understand how God chose me. I am thankful to have come to the realization that he chose me to encourage and to have empathy for those in need. Chosen by my heavenly Father for this day, month, and year! Chosen!

Thank you, Jesus, for choosing me!

CHOSEN BY GOD

Thoughts & Reflections

Photo Credit: Tanya Y. Hines

"Likewise, the tongue is a small part of the body, but it makes great boasts. Consider what a great forest is set on fire by a small spark."

—JAMES 1:26 (NIV)

Final Thoughts

"Faith in the Midst" is intended to inspire you to have strong faith as you encounter your own personal life challenges. As I have shared some of my experiences, I understand that there are so many other struggles we can potentially face that can run the gamut from addictions, gambling, sexual identity issues, infidelity, abuse, job loss, faithlessness, hopelessness, sickness, decision making, the death of children and other loved ones, and so on. As I stated earlier in the book, life truly happens to everyone. There is no escaping it. The Lord says in (John 16:33 NIV), "I have told you these things, so that in me you may have peace. In this world you will have trouble. But take heart! I have overcome the world." He's saying, my son, my daughter, if you are in this world, there is an enemy that you will have to contend with. That enemy's main purpose is to bring you grief, sorrow, pain and trouble. He is good at his job, and he won't ever stop trying to trip you up and cause you to lose your faith. That's his main objective, but God consistently reminds us not to lose our peace and faith and not to be overcome, because the Lord has overcome all the tricks the enemy can pull out of his little old trick bag. Keep fighting for your faith as you come up against life challenges.

A strong faith will defeat the enemy every time. The enemy cannot stand up against faith and those who believe that their father in heaven is greater than the problems they face here on earth.

In the center of the struggle, we must trust the promise that God has not forsaken us. God has not taken his eyes off you, not even for a moment. His love and concern for you is detailed: *"And even the very hairs of your head are all numbered"* (Matthew 10:30 NIV); *"Indeed, the very hairs of your head are all numbered. Don't be afraid; you are worth more than many sparrows"* (Luke 12:7 NIV). Can you even imagine counting your child's or spouse's hairs on their head because you love them and are that concerned about their every detail? Well, our heavenly Father loves you just that much. That is a kind of love that empowers us to become bold in our faith and spiritual stance. It also promotes a trust that no matter what life may bring, my God is always right there watching over me, holding me, and carrying me when I need carrying. It provides an assurance in our faith to know that we do not battle life alone: (John 4:4 NIV), states "You, dear children, are from God and have overcome them, because the one who is in you is greater than the one who is in the world." Who is in you? God. Who is in the world? The enemy. Who did God say in his Word is greater? You are indeed greater because of Christ that lives in you is the greatest! Greater than anything that may try to knock you down. Greater than anything that the enemy can throw at you, but you and I must always remember that our strength to stand is not our own but the Lord's. Our mind, thoughts, and actions must always reflect what God has said and done on our behalf. I don't in any manner trivialize life and all that we deal with. As you've read in my mini faith chapters, I've dealt with some giants, but I cannot stress enough that faith is the giant destroyer. Where you place your focus, be it in God or in the problem can make the difference in how you persevere through the situation. If the focus on God becomes greater than the focus on the problem, this can be the difference between one's victory and one's defeat, depending on your mindset and level of faith. Remember, faith is a mountain mover. Faith is a demon killer and a spiritual motivator.

FAITH IN THE MIDST

Faith is a confidence builder, a spiritual weapon and pleasing to God. It is confidence in God that is essential to facing your giants." Faith is victory's comrade: (Matthew 9:29 NIV), "Then he touched their eyes and said, 'According to your faith will it be done to you."

Keep the Faith...

FINAL THOUGHTS & REFLECTIONS

Photo Credit: Gregory Hines

Through it all, I choose to continue to praise and trust God!

ABOUT THE AUTHOR

Tanya Y. Hines uses her gifts to engage in the ministry of encouragement. Through her personal photos and inspirational writing, she uplifts, encourages, and motivates others. Tanya treasures her faith and knows it has helped her through some of her toughest moments. By honestly and authentically sharing her trials, she hopes to offer her readers hope as they encounter their own life challenges.

Her desire is to embolden others to always walk with trust in the Lord, even in those deep, dark moments of despair and hopelessness. Giving all praise to the Lord, the rock of her salvation, Tanya prays that her books will bless others. When she is not writing or serving in ministry, she enjoys spending quality time with her husband and college-age son.

CONTACT INFORMATION:

To schedule Tanya Y. Hines
for workshops, conferences, and speaking engagements email:
jesusthruthelens@gmail.com

www.ingramcontent.com/pod-product-compliance
Lightning Source LLC
Chambersburg PA
CBHW072020290426
44109CB00018B/2299